50 Years

of mac

A Half Century of British Life

Stan McMurtry mac

Edited by Mark Bryant

ROBINSON

First published in Great Britain in 2018 by Robinson

3 5 7 9 10 8 6 4 2

Cartoons and Introduction copyright © Stan McMurtry, 2018

Selection and texts copyright © Mark Bryant, 2018

'The Rain in Spain' is a song from the musical *My Fair Lady*. Book and lyrics by
Alan Jay Lerner, music by Frederick Loewe. ©MTI Enterprises, Inc.

The moral rights of the authors have been asserted.

A CIP catalogue record for this is available from the British Library.

ISBN 978-1-47214-162-0

Printed and bound in Great Britain by Bell & Bain Ltd

Papers used by Robinson are from well-manged forests and
other responsible sources.

Robinson
An imprint of Little, Brown Book Group
Carmelite House, 50 Victoria Embankment
London EC4Y 0DZ

An Hachette UK Company

www.littlebrown.co.uk

This book is dedicated to my darling wife, Liz.
The bravest and kindest woman I've ever known.

Introduction

Almost exactly fifty years ago, a young man clutching a drawing pad and a few pencils walked into Northcliffe House, near Fleet Street in London, to start the first day of a trial period as the social and political cartoonist of the *Daily Sketch*, a tabloid owned and run at that time by Associated Newspapers. That nervous, quivering jelly was me and I remember so well just how terrified I was at the prospect of having to dream up what I hoped would be an amusing comment on that day's news.

The resident cartoonist was retiring due to ill health and three other hopefuls and I had been invited to try for the job. We were each to have our work published for two days and then a decision would be made on who would be taken on.

Amazingly, without having had to bribe anyone, I was given a six-month trial. It was a huge turning point in my career. Little did I know then that I would still be providing the daily cartoon fifty years later.

The job with the *Daily Sketch*, however, was to last only two years. The paper was closed down and taken over by its sister paper in the group, the *Daily Mail*, and, much to my delight, I was taken on with it.

For me, they have been fifty great years. I have been lucky enough to work for two editorial giants of journalism: David English, later to become Sir David English, and Paul Dacre, both possessing a really good sense of humour and the ability to sort the wheat from the chaff when presented with my daily bundle of rough ideas for selection.

Looking back, it's hard to believe that I have been keeping ink and board manufacturers in business for so long. Not once has it been boring. The news changes constantly from day to day, so there is always some new topic to chew over and develop into an idea for the next day's paper. Each day is a fresh challenge, and every morning the ritual is performed of scanning rival papers to see what one's fellow cartoonists have made of the same subjects that each of us had been struggling with the day before.

Lots of readers collect cartoon originals and once in a while a celebrity or a politician who might have appeared in one of the drawings gets in touch asking to buy or to be given the work. Over my fifty years tenure I've handed over originals to The Beatles, Frank Sinatra, Laurence Olivier, Ted Heath, Harold Wilson, Margaret Thatcher, Denis Healey and countless others. I have been asked to draw for Dustin Hoffman and Roger Moore, Eric Morecambe and Ernie Wise and if this all sounds conceited then I'm sorry. I don't mean it to be. I just thought that you, the reader, might be interested.

Being a newspaper cartoonist doesn't mean that one is always tied to a drawing board, although most days it does mean exactly that. Occasionally, wonderful diversions happen. I have been sent to a nudist colony, where I had to strip off in order to present a drawing to a group of nudists. There was the time I was challenged by the Army Catering Corps to compete with a squad of young and fit soldiers over their assault course after they complained when I had drawn them as fat and spotty. That was hard work and exhausting, but I managed to finish the course without having a heart attack, and it was a really fun day. On another occasion, I was treated to a slap-up, and very boozy, lunch by the famous American film star John Wayne in his hotel suite.

These joyous events don't occur every week, but just once in a while they do, and I count myself a very lucky scribbler that I have experienced so many of them.

On top of all that good fortune I have been awarded the title 'Cartoonist of the Year' several times and no, I did not bribe any of the judges!

Then a few years ago came the icing on the cake. I was asked to make my way to Buckingham Palace to be given an MBE by Her Majesty the Queen. Just how lucky can you get?

Regular readers of the *Daily Mail* probably know that for many years I have drawn within each cartoon a small sketch of my wife Liz's face. She's always there hidden somewhere in the daily drawing, perhaps in the pattern of a curtain or in a tree in the background. She has become so popular that I get sent cuttings of the paper by readers if they have been unable to find her, asking me to pinpoint exactly where she is hidden.

Sadly, my darling Liz passed away in 2017 having suffered with that most dreadful of afflictions, motor neurone disease. So, in memory of her, I continue to put her in the drawing every day. Here is a selection of those drawings (she only appears in the later ones), from the 1960s right up to 2018. I do hope you'll enjoy looking back over the years and perhaps even enjoy the odd chuckle as you do so.

One of MAC's earliest editorial cartoons for the *Daily Sketch* to bear the MAC logo, this drawing comments on the wartime singer Vera Lynn, known as 'The Forces' Sweetheart', who received an OBE from the Queen in 1969.

More than one hundred hippie squatters moved into an empty sixty-room mansion between Buckingham Palace and Hyde Park which was scheduled for demolition. They were later evicted by police.

'Right, luv. One more chorus of "We'll Meet Again" and we'll let you go and collect your OBE.'
Daily Sketch, 12 February 1969

'Here's your cup of sugar – 'is Royal 'ighness wants to know when he can have his electric drill back.'
Daily Sketch, 17 September 1969

When London refuse collectors began an unofficial strike in support of a wage claim there were worries for public health as streets filled with piles of rubbish which attracted rats and large 'super flies'.

Singer and actor Frank Sinatra announced his retirement in 1971. However, it was short-lived as he returned in 1973 with a television special and a new album entitled *Ol' Blue Eyes Is Back*.

'Well, there aren't any super flies around our bin.'
Daily Sketch, 8 October 1969

'Sure, I've retired – but I still like you guys around in case I feel like a song in the bath.'
Daily Sketch, 25 March 1971

The Conservative Government under Edward Heath unveiled plans to ease traffic congestion in cities by establishing park-and-ride schemes and introducing tougher parking restrictions for car users.

'. . . and if you haven't moved the bits in two minutes we get really nasty!'

20 January 1973

Labour won the General Election of February 1974. After the first budget of new Chancellor Denis Healey in March, which had postponed the threatened introduction of a wealth tax to 'soak the rich', there were fears about what his 'mini-budget' in July would contain.

'Good heavens, is it that time already? – We've missed the Chancellor's speech!'
22 July 1974

Prime Minister Harold Wilson called a second General Election in October 1974 and at the State Opening of Parliament the newspapers were full of stories about his business affairs. Some of his private documents went missing in a series of burglaries which he believed were part of a smear campaign by anti-Labour media.

'. . . and my total earnings for 1973–4 were . . . oh, dear. I seem to have someone's tax forms mixed up with my speech.' *29 October 1974*

Having lost the General Election, Edward Heath was replaced as Conservative leader by former Education Secretary, Margaret Thatcher, who became the first woman ever to lead a political party in Britain. Her 'stepping stones' are (right to left): Heath, Geoffrey Howe, Edward du Cann, Jim Prior and Willie Whitelaw.

One Small Step for Woman – A Giant Leap for Womankind
12 February 1975

Skateboarding, originally developed in the USA as a form of 'sidewalk surfing' for Californian surfers when waves were flat, became increasingly popular in the UK in the 1970s. For safety reasons young skateboarders were encouraged to wear bicycle helmets to reduce the risk of head injuries.

5 January 1978

As the NHS marked its thirtieth anniversary, there was widespread criticism of unofficial industrial action taken by some hospital telephonists (who were dissatisfied with their recent pay settlement) who pulled out plugs and claimed to know which cases were urgent and which were not.

'The switchboard operator at the hospital says take two aspirins and stop wasting her time.'
10 March 1978

Work on the Thames Barrier (begun in 1974) was largely complete by 1982. Its flood gates were designed to protect Greater London from high tides and storm surges.

'Oi! Do you know how much those gates going up and down costs?'
9 November 1982

The whole nation was shocked by the sudden death of Eric Morecambe, aged 58, shortly after he had appeared on stage in Tewkesbury, Gloucestershire. He was widely regarded as one of the funniest and best-loved comedians of the 20th century. This drawing was reproduced on the programme for his memorial service.

You brought us sunshine, you brought us laughter, you brought us love . . .
29 May 1984

In a speech at Hampton Court Palace to mark the 150th anniversary of the Royal Institute of British Architects, Prince Charles criticised the proposed National Gallery extension in Trafalgar Square as 'a monstrous carbuncle on the face of a well-loved and elegant friend'.

'For heaven's sake, Charles! He's only a child!'

1 June 1984

In an interview for BBC TV, Prince Charles publicly confessed that he talked to his plants.

'. . . then, when one discovers the mirror within oneself reflecting the
fundamental meaning of life, one . . .' *23 September 1986*

Health inspectors who descended on the kitchens of the prestigious Dorchester Hotel in London's Park Lane discovered one ingredient that was not on the menu … cockroaches.

'Oh dear, I thought they'd got rid of the cockroaches . . .'
24 November 1988

In response to a crisis in consumer confidence which had been generated by a series of food scares including salmonella in eggs and listeria in cheese, the Food Safety Advisory Centre (FSAC) was established in the UK in February 1989.

'First it became unsafe to have cigarettes, then sex, then food, then water – so I thought, what's left?' *10 February 1989*

A court heard how a James Bond-style ultrasonic gun disguised as a pair of binoculars had been used to stun a top thoroughbred during a race at Ascot. The high-pitched sound caused the horse to veer suddenly and throw the jockey as they were heading for victory.

'Of course they're just ordinary binoculars, sir, but could we have a look?'

2 November 1989

After twenty-seven years in prison in South Africa, anti-apartheid campaigner Nelson Mandela walked to freedom on 11 February 1990. He was later the country's first black head of state and served as President of South Africa from 1994 to 1999.

'After 27 years it's lovely having a man about the house again, Nelson.'

13 February 1990

Worries that BSE or 'mad cow disease' could spread to humans led to a Government clamp-down on meat products. At the same time, to reassure the public, Conservative Agriculture Minister, John Gummer, and his four-year-old daughter ate beefburgers in front of the British media.

'It's not as bad as I feared – she's only got "extremely silly cow disease".'

15 May 1990

On 22 July 1990, Nick Faldo won the British Open Golf Championships at St Andrews, Scotland, for the second time. On 23 July, Margaret Thatcher (whose husband Denis was a great golf fan) finalised her summer reshuffle . . .

'I see she's started on her reshuffle . . .'

23 July 1990

Aliens? Hoaxers? The 'Eastfield Pictogram' spotted in a field in Alton Barnes near Devizes, Wiltshire, led to a new era of interest in the study of crop circles, which mostly appeared in the summer in the south-west of England.

'Haven't you got anywhere else but Wiltshire?'

27 July 1990

Unofficial strikes on North Sea oil rigs, combined with increasing nervousness about the situation in oil-rich Kuwait, which had been invaded and occupied by Iraqi forces under President Saddam Hussein, led to fuel shortages at home.

'It's His Lordship, M'Lady – don't smoke near the swimming-pool, he's filled it with petrol . . .'

7 August 1990

As multinational troops, led by the USA, mustered on the Kuwait/Saudi border in preparation for Operation Desert Storm and the beginning of the Gulf War, temperatures in Britain soared for the Bank Holiday weekend.

'I sure hope there's no action before Tuesday, Sarge – the Brits insist on having their Bank Holiday.' *27 August 1990*

Britain and France were united for the first time since the Ice Age when a two-inch (50 mm) borehole 14 miles (22.5 kilometres) from the Kent coast joined up with the French Chunnellers, allowing through a 'whiff of garlic'. Mrs Thatcher's negative stance on Europe, however, cast a shadow.

'*Sacre bleu!* It is wet concrete! Zey have bunged up their side again!'
1 November 1990

Margaret Thatcher, the longest-serving British Prime Minister of the 20th century, resigned. Foreign Secretary Douglas Hurd and Chancellor John Major threw their hats into the ring (Major won).

Who's Big Enough?
23 November 1990

Buckingham Palace announced that the Prince of Wales would make a two-day morale-boosting visit to the 15,000-strong British task force stationed in the Gulf.

'I'm sure it's him – he's just wished that cactus a happy Christmas.'

20 December 1990

The *Sunday Times* attacked the younger royals for 'parading a mixture of upper-class decadence and insensitivity' with regard to the Gulf War, as media reports showed them skiing, pheasant hunting, golfing and partying at nightclubs.

'Thank you, Ma'am, but honestly, we feel the Royal Family is doing quite enough for the war effort . . .' *12 February 1991*

British Rail was heavily criticised when 65 per cent of trains failed due to the 'wrong type of snow'. Even the new multi-million-pound InterCity 225 'super-trains' were hit when the powder-like snow blocked their air-intakes.

'No, you can't speak to the station master! Due to a design fault his air-intake has been blocked by snow.' *14 February 1991*

More than 120,000 people, including the Prince and Princess of Wales, attended a televised open-air free concert in London's Hyde Park to celebrate 55-year-old Italian tenor Luciano Pavarotti's thirty years as an opera star.

'Sure, honey . . . for £300 we got darned good seats – but I've always thought Pavarotti was a big guy with a beard.' *30 July 1991*

British Rail announced that it would be reopening a number of little-used stations on branch lines across the country.

'British Rail is pleased to announce the re-opening of the Great Twissington-on-Crouch railway station – your next train is due in approximately . . .' *1 August 1991*

The 24-year-old daughter of a Buckingham Palace clerk, living in the Royal Mews, was arrested following a police investigation into a drugs ring.

'Well, they don't normally behave like this after a Bob Martin's conditioning powder . . .'

22 October 1991

The performance of John Major in the discussions which led to the Maastricht Treaty on the formation of the European Union had a mixed reception in the UK. Some critics even drew parallels with Neville Chamberlain's return from the pre-war Munich conference to appease Adolf Hitler.

Peace in Our Time
12 December 1991

Company magazine revealed that in a recent survey 37 per cent of men questioned had been sexually harassed by female managers and some had been promised better work prospects if they slept with their female boss.

'Attention, everybody! I'm looking for a new head of department . . .'
11 February 1992

After 151 years, *Punch* magazine closed on 8 April 1992, with losses running at more than £1 million a year and circulation down from 175,000 to 33,000. (It was revived in 1996 but finally closed in 2002.)

'I suppose they're trying their best, but I'm going to miss *Punch*.'

26 March 1992

The notorious Hole-in-the-Wall 'ram-raiders' gang struck for the fifth time, using a stolen JCB to scoop an Abbey National cash-machine containing £55,000 at Hempstead in Kent.

'I told you not to stop at the lights!'
21 April 1992

Conservative Health Secretary Virginia Bottomley announced plans to introduce on-the-spot fines for offenders in non-smoking areas in an attempt to make 80 per cent of public places smoke-free within a year.

'Oi . . .!'

28 January 1993

To try to understand the rise in youth crime in Britain, the Home Office published the report of a new survey, *Young People and Crime, 1992–1993*, which investigated the reasons why some young people start to offend.

'This one's a bit far-fetched. A kid has to call his teacher "Sir", nicks something, gets a thick ear from a copper and is sent home to find his employed parents are in and not at the pub . . .' *22 February 1993*

After years of debate, Conservative Transport Secretary John MacGregor finally decided on the route the Channel Tunnel link-line would take through Kent, terminating at St Pancras station in London.

'Good news! The Channel Tunnel rail link isn't coming this way after all.'

23 March 1993

The NutraSweet London Marathon was won by 34-year-old
Ford worker Eamonn Martin from Basildon, Essex, in 2 hours
10 mins 50 secs. It was his first marathon. Others were slower.

'We'll let him go another five miles then nab him for kerb-crawling.'

19 April 1993

The Council for the Protection of Rural England announced that 27,500 acres (11,129 hectares) of English countryside are lost to urban planners and road-builders each year.

'Do you realise that 27,000 acres of countryside are disappearing under concrete every year in England?' *30 July 1993*

Conservative Home Secretary Michael Howard called for 'vigilance, not vigilantes'
as a Gallup survey revealed that public confidence in the police was at such
a low ebb that 76 per cent of those polled could consider becoming vigilantes.

'I do hope this doesn't mean an end to your valuable work for
Neighbourhood Watch, Miss Penthrope . . .' *11 August 1993*

A giant West African snail, 10in (25.4cm) long and weighing 9oz (255g), was found by a groundsman at a holiday centre in Devon. It had presumably been left behind by visitors.

'Typical man! We're flooded out and all you can worry about is a snail getting at your cabbages!' *15 October 1993*

A blue budgerigar owned by an 81-year-old woman from South Bank,
near Middlesbrough – who had smoked 40 cigarettes a day for sixty-four years –
was reported as the first bird victim of lung cancer by passive smoking.

'Honestly, Doctor, I'm trying to kick the habit – I'm down to ten budgies a week.'

28 January 1994

A number of Tory sex scandals rocked John Major's government.
Meanwhile, Edvard Munch's famous painting, *The Scream*, was
stolen from the National Gallery in Oslo, Norway.

The Scream
14 February 1994

As the Queen prepared for her first visit to Russia forensic tests on human remains proved conclusively that Tsar Nicholas II, George V's first cousin, had been murdered.

'Why not let bygones be bygones when you go, dear? President Yeltsin had nothing to do with your grandfather's cousin . . .' *18 February 1994*

Engineers monitoring subsidence from tunnelling work on the nearby Jubilee line Underground extension discovered that the world's most famous clock-tower, Westminster's 320-foot (97.5 metres) tall Big Ben, had shifted 0.07 in (2mm) in a fortnight.

'The time? Certainly, sir. It's half-past three.'

1 November 1994

Actress Joanna Lumley, who played the flamboyant, champagne-drinking character, Patsy, in BBC TV's award-winning comedy series, *Absolutely Fabulous*, received an OBE at Buckingham Palace.

'I expect it was Absolutely Fabulous meeting Joanna Lumley, wasn't it, darling? Darling?'
4 May 1995

The VE-Day celebrations in Britain included nationwide street parties and a huge festival in Hyde Park featuring a Veterans' Centre equipped with a computer-linked search facility to help reunite old wartime comrades.

'Remind me, Albert. How did I sneak through the German lines in 1944?'

9 May 1995

Various members of the Royal Family have asked MAC for the originals of his cartoons over the years, but he was especially pleased to have a request for this one from Her Majesty when security was tightened dramatically in 1996.

'I feel sorry for the corgis.'
27 February 1996

Labour's Deputy PM John Prescott and Heritage Secretary Chris Smith attacked the fat cats running the Lottery and the recently privatised utilities as profits continued to soar when services dwindled and household bills increased.

The Gravy Train
6 June 1997

Labour's Deputy Prime Minister, John Prescott, unveiled his
plans for an integrated transport policy aimed at encouraging
the use of public transport systems.

'Thought I'd give this public transport thing a try. Tell the chauffeur chappie to drop me off at my club,
hang about, then pick me up again about six . . .' *22 August 1997*

Singer and actor Frank Sinatra, 'Ol' Blue Eyes', died aged 82 in Los Angeles, California. He was the last of the infamous hell-raising 'Rat Pack' of showbusiness friends which also included Dean Martin, Sammy Davis Jr. and Peter Lawford.

'You just missed it. Man, what a party – the Rat Pack are together again.'

18 May 1998

The Times serialised a new book by KGB defector Vasili Mitrokhin, in which it was revealed that Melita Norwood, an 87-year-old suburban great-grandmother, had been a Russian spy for four decades.

'Do you suppose our Miss Featherstone has ever worked for the Russians?
She's been very jumpy over the past few days.' *13 September 1999*

The year's shortlist for the annual £20,000 Turner Prize for modern art included *My Bed*, featuring 36-year-old artist Tracey Emin's own bed, complete with soiled sheets and underwear, cigarette ends, empty vodka bottles and old newspapers.

'Wake up, Norman. You've been nominated for the Turner Prize.'

22 October 1999

Tory leader William Hague's claims in *GQ* magazine that he drank 14 pints of beer a day as a teenager, while working as a delivery man for a drinks company in South Yorkshire, were treated with scepticism in some quarters.

'Oh, Norman. I'm so proud. I think our Kevin's going into politics.'
11 August 2000

The London Eye, 443 feet (135 metres) high and then the biggest revolving wheel in the world, was finally lifted into its upright position on the south bank of the Thames, nearly opposite the Houses of Parliament.

'Damn! It's still not moving – Cyril, six more sacks of hamsters.'

18 October 2000

The row about the Royal Family and bloodsports was reignited when the Queen was photographed wringing the neck of a pheasant injured during a shoot at Sandringham.

'Don't worry. You've got five seconds' start and if it's not a clean shot my wife wrings your neck.'
20 November 2000

Inspired by the film *Billy Elliot* – in which a working-class boy becomes a star ballet dancer – Labour Education Secretary David Blunkett pledged £35 million to fund after-school classes in dance, drama and music for deprived inner-city children.

'Aye. I'm bloody ashamed of him. He wants to be a miner.'

13 February 2001

After a significant rise in attacks on NATO planes patrolling the 'no-fly zones' in Iraq, US and British aircraft bombed Baghdad. Meanwhile, a book was published listing the 'accidental wit' of US President George W. Bush.

'There's some guy called Blair on the phone. Is he the one I'm bombing or do I have to be polite?'
19 February 2001

A major outbreak of foot-and-mouth disease led to the destruction of more than 6 million cows and sheep in Britain. In an effort to prevent the spread of further contagion, Labour Agriculture Minister, Nick Brown, announced that the Army might have to be called in to help control the crisis.

'Marjorie. Some people are here about your sore foot.'
13 March 2001

The Duke and Duchess of Wessex – who had referred to the Queen as 'the old dear' – were summoned to Buckingham Palace after it was claimed that they were using tax-payer-funded state visits to drum up business for Prince Edward's ailing TV company, Ardent.

'Edward. Can you and Sophie pop round again? The old dear would like another word.'

6 April 2001

Labour Deputy Prime Minister John Prescott punched a countryside protester in the face and became involved in a brawl after he was hit by an egg on his way to address a meeting in Rhyl, North Wales.

mac

This cartoon was going to poke fun at John Prescott. But I want to keep my teeth – MAC.

18 May 2001

Following the resignation of William Hague, Shadow Chancellor Michael Portillo announced his candidacy in the Tory leadership race. Other contenders included Shadow Defence Secretary Iain Duncan Smith, former Chancellor Kenneth Clarke, right-winger David Davis and Party Chairman Michael Ancram.

'Today you've got one Napoleon, a woman who thinks she's a sausage, a mad axeman and some poor souls who want to lead the Tory Party.' *18 June 2001*

Using the latest technology, Professor John Burland, a British civil engineer from Imperial College, London, helped to stabilise the famous 14th-century Leaning Tower of Pisa in Italy, which had been close to collapse.

'You're right. It *is* Viagra.'

19 June 2001

Scotland Yard announced that it would be issuing 'Taser' electronic stun-guns to the police. The US-made guns used laser-targeted darts to deliver a 50,000-volt shock capable of temporarily paralysing victims and had a range of 20 feet (6 metres).

'Golly gosh, Sarge. You're pretty fast. Another split second and he would have fouled the pavement.'

2 August 2001

French police reported that they had eventually captured forty-four asylum-seekers who had managed to walk 7 miles (11 km) into the Channel Tunnel.

'Quickly, Mohammad. Quickly! Put another leaf on the line.'
3 September 2001

As anthrax cases in the US began to rise, the British government revealed that it only had enough stock of the antidote drug doxycycline to treat two million people. (This cartoon is also owned by the Queen.)

'Don't drink that one, Mother. It's our anti-anthrax vaccine.'
16 October 2001

Rail commuters already suffering from dismal services – compounded by a series of regional strikes by unions – were incensed when train operators announced huge fare rises on hundreds of routes. Labour's Europe Minister, Peter Hain, interviewed in the *Spectator* magazine, conceded that Britain now had 'the worst railways in Europe'.

'We did it, folks. We finally did it! – worst in Europe!'
11 January 2002

There were fears for passenger safety when a major computer glitch at the National Air Traffic Control Services headquarters in Swanwick, Hampshire – the second within two weeks – caused widespread chaos and the delay or cancellation of 700 UK flights affecting 150,000 air travellers.

'We apologise to passengers for the severe delays. Rest assured our engineers are working flat out to trace the computer fault . . .' *11 April 2002*

The celebrations to mark the Queen's Golden Jubilee included a pop music concert at Buckingham Palace attended by 12,000 people, with many more outside watching on giant screens. The following day there was a ceremonial procession from Buckingham Palace to St Paul's Cathedral.

'Only 9 hours, 35 minutes and eleven seconds to go . . .'

4 June 2002

The time difference between Japan and the UK meant that the quarter-final match between England and Brazil in the football World Cup was broadcast early in the morning. Nonetheless, 30 million British viewers tuned in (Brazil won 2-1).

'You were sleeping so soundly that we didn't want to wake you – do you want to know the score?'

21 June 2002

Britain was put on a war footing as Labour Prime Minister Tony Blair met President Bush for talks on Saddam Hussein and Iraq. Meanwhile, fugitive terrorist leader Osama bin Laden remained in hiding in Afghanistan and record numbers of asylum seekers from Iraq and Afghanistan led to a backlog in the processing of applications.

'Don't worry. By the time they've processed our asylum applications the bombing will be over and we can go home.' *3 September 2002*

One of the proposals made at the Conservative Party Conference in Bournemouth was to expand the 'right to buy' scheme for council tenants, introduced in the 1980s, to include the million or so people who then lived in housing-association properties.

'Fantastic news. If the Tories get in we can buy this place.'
10 October 2002

The 29-year-old British No.2 tennis player, Greg Rusedski, crashed out of Wimbledon and faced a large fine after swearing (on live TV) at the umpire who had failed to call for a point to be replayed after a spectator falsely called a ball out.

'I say! Anyone for f****** tennis?'

27 June 2003

The position of Tony Blair's chief spin doctor, Alastair Campbell, seemed to be in jeopardy after allegations were made by a BBC correspondent that he had 'sexed up' intelligence reports in order to get the British public behind the war with Iraq.

'Are you still there? . . . don't go, Alastair . . . please, Alastair . . . ALASTAIR!'
30 June 2003

As the number of speed cameras increased throughout Britain, there was widespread criticism of police priorities, especially when it was revealed that police in Scarborough, Yorkshire, had taken two and a half hours to respond to a 999 call.

'Sorry for the delay in answering your 999 call, madam. This is due to us being absolutely overwhelmed by paperwork.' *19 August 2003*

A Channel 4 drama-documentary, *The Deal*, alleged that in 1994 Tony Blair and Gordon Brown had met in the Granita restaurant in Islington and agreed that Brown would succeed him as Prime Minister if Labour came to power.

New Deal
1 October 2003

The RMS *Queen Mary 2*, then the world's biggest cruise ship – it was 1132 feet (345 metres) long – was officially named by the Queen at a rain-soaked ceremony in Southampton prior to setting off on her maiden voyage to Florida, USA.

'Great news. The front end of the ship has reached Florida and it's sunny!'
9 January 2004

A survey revealed that the cost of the male mid-life crisis had rocketed in recent years with men in their 40s and 50s now spending £2 billion a year on cosmetic treatment, psychiatric counselling, motorcycles and even plastic surgery.

'He's had psychiatry, surgery, botox injections and bought himself a motorbike – nip out and tell him his toupee's still in his helmet.' *22 April 2004*

Heavy rain stopped play during the Wimbledon tennis tournament, reminding
commentators of the cloudburst during a match in 1996 which led Sir Cliff
Richard to begin his famous impromptu singalong with spectators.

'How bad does it have to get before they let Cliff Richard out?'

24 June 2004

A report by Adair Turner, head of the Government's Pensions Commission, said that to plug the £57 billion black hole in public and private pensions provision, men and women would have to delay their retirement ages to 70 and 67, respectively.

'Damn! He's got away!'

14 October 2004

At a meeting of EU interior ministers in Luxembourg, Labour Home Secretary David Blunkett agreed to sign away Britain's power to veto new European laws on immigration and asylum but insisted that this would not affect UK border controls.

'Of course we'll still retain control of our bord . . .'

26 October 2004

A Home Office survey revealed that three-quarters of Britain's criminals are never caught, only one in 100 ever goes to trial, violent crime had increased by 6 per cent and gun crime was up by 5 per cent.

'I'm just popping down to the bank. Is there anything you want from the shops?'

27 January 2005

In an attempt to stem rising school drop-out rates and improve literacy, Labour Chancellor Gordon Brown unveiled new Education Maintenance Allowances of £75 a week to encourage youngsters to stay in full-time education or training.

'I bet it says fags are up again.'

17 March 2005

As the crisis in Britain's hospitals deepened, Labour leaders claimed that Conservative election plans for the health service would result in patients paying huge sums for treatment and threaten the very existence of the NHS itself.

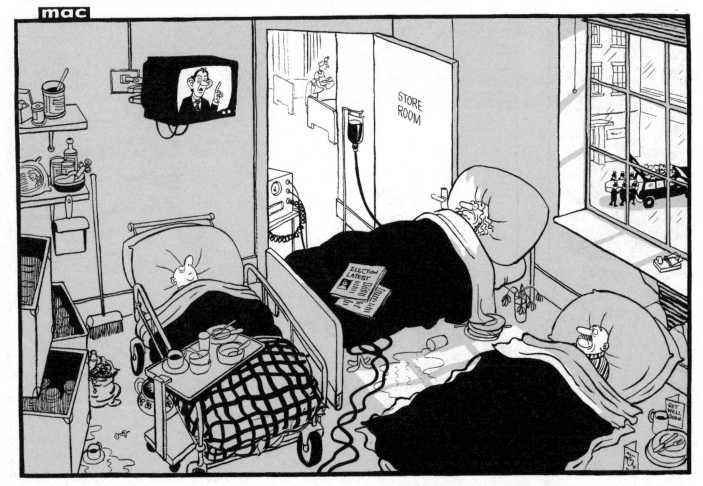

'Remember, folks. Voting for the Conservatives would mean an end to the NHS as we know it.'

19 April 2005

After the leaking of the Attorney-General's report on the legality of the invasion of Iraq, Tony Blair and Labour leaders were accused of lying to the British people over the reasons for going to war, a claim they denied strenuously.

'Good morning, young lady. I'm so pleased to meet you in your beautiful home and hey! What a lovely little doggy . . .' *28 April 2005*

Aged 62, wrinkly rocker Sir Mick Jagger and the Rolling Stones kicked off their latest world tour – estimated to earn them £10 million each – with a sell-out concert at Boston's Fenway Park baseball stadium.

'I think I've pulled. Mick's asked me back to his place for cocoa and a digestive biscuit.'

24 August 2005

As the debate over the wisdom of allowing 24-hour drinking continued, the Government introduced a 'Britishness' test for immigrants who wished to apply for a British passport.

'Congratulations, Mr Sajeed. You've passed the Government's Britishness test.'

1 November 2005

The Queen celebrated her 80th birthday.
She received more than 20,000 birthday cards.

'If that's the post, Philip, dear, will you see if there are any cards for me?'

21 April 2006

It was announced that a Sussex woman, who would be 63 in September, was seven months pregnant after receiving fertility treatment in Italy.

'Damn! Have you ever walked into a room then forgotten what you came in for?'

5 May 2006

The National Farmers' Union and a number of academics backed
claims made by West Country cheesemakers that cows moo with
regional accents depending on which part of Britain they live in.

'Thanks for the elocution lessons but I think I preferred them mooing with a Brummie accent.'

24 August 2006

A 31-year-old Iraqi man who lost his sight in a bomb blast in his homeland became the first blind person in the UK to be convicted of dangerous driving. Arrested in the West Midlands he had been given instructions on braking and turning by a passenger.

'Okay, relax. It isn't that blind bloke driving again. It's his guide dog.'

6 September 2006

Tony Blair made his last Labour Party Conference speech. Meanwhile, in an attempt to crack down on the huge increase in the domestic production of cannabis since its reclassification as a Class C drug, police forces raided addresses in England and Wales.

'Well, honestly. Blair's last conference speech and not a word about legalising cannabis factories to supplement pensions.' *27 September 2006*

A 55-year-old British Airways employee, who had worn a tiny Christian cross around her neck to work for seven years, took the airline to court over its new regulations which insisted that all personal items should be worn under the BA uniform.

'Y'know, British Airways are right. A cross does look better worn under the uniform.'

22 November 2006

Dame Helen Mirren won the award for Best Actress at Hollywood's
Golden Globe Awards for her role in the film *The Queen* about the life
of Elizabeth II. (She later also won an Oscar for the part.)

'How terribly exciting, Philip, dear. They're making a film called *Helen Mirren*
and I've been offered the part.' *17 January 2007*

In another 'Frankenstein food' case, which British watchdog officials described as 'very disturbing', a California-based company was given US government approval to grow test crops of rice which had been genetically modified with human DNA.

'Aaaaaaaaaaaaaaaaaaaargh!'

7 March 2007

At his last Prime Minister's Question Time, Tony Blair was given an unprecedented standing ovation by Labour and Tory MPs. Meanwhile, a monsoon-like downpour led to widespread flooding as more rain fell in 24 hours than the average for the whole of June.

'. . . and so, as a fitting end to his ten glorious years, Tony Blair walks triumphantly off into the sunset . . .'

28 June 2007

A judge in Manchester condemned police for wasting tax-payers' money when it was revealed in court that a 12-year-old boy, who had thrown a cocktail sausage at a pensioner during an argument, had been arrested and charged with common assault.

'Be careful, Sarge. He's got a sausage!'
24 August 2007

Labour Justice Secretary Jack Straw proposed an amendment to the Criminal Justice and Immigration Bill to allow citizens to use 'reasonable force' in self-defence against burglars and other criminals.

'You fool! The violence my husband is about to administer comes with the full authority of Jack Straw.' *28 September 2007*

When a 68-year-old animal behaviourist from East Sussex developed crippling arthritis in her back, she trained her Newfoundland dog to work the washing machine, help with housework and carry shopping bags.

'. . . and another thing. Next door's dog does the laundry, tidies up and brings the shopping home!'

4 January 2008

After admitting that she did not feel safe walking the streets of London after dark, Labour Home Secretary Jacqui Smith tried to make amends by saying that she had bought a kebab one evening in Peckham. It was later revealed that she'd had a police escort.

'Please stop screaming, Home Secretary. The man in the shop is supposed to have a knife.'

22 January 2008

Reports by the Royal Institution of Chartered Surveyors and others revealed that the housing market was at its worst for thirty years with one in three estate agents facing closure within the next twelve months.

'Oh yes. I come down here most mornings to feed the estate agents.'

15 April 2008

The *Daily Telegraph* revealed that a Conservative MP had claimed £1600 to construct a floating island – complete with a miniature house modelled on an 18th-century Swedish building – on a lake in his Hampshire home to keep his ducks safe from foxes.

'Make the most of this. Our man is being forced to stand down at the next election.'

22 May 2009

Around the world millions watched the wedding of Prince William and Kate Middleton at Westminster Abbey. Meanwhile, in the World Snooker Championship at the Crucible in Sheffield, John Higgins beat Ronnie O'Sullivan in a tense quarter-finals match.

'Would anyone mind if I switched over to the snooker?'
29 April 2011

The BBC announced that it would make £1.3 billion in cuts,
including reducing BBC1's TV programme budget by £35 million
and relocating 1000 jobs to Salford, near Manchester.

'Well, that was the news – and now a joke about a parrot, a nun and a one-legged camel . . .'

7 October 2011

A French silent film, *The Artist*, won three awards at the 69th Golden Globes ceremony in Beverly Hills, California, but the show was stolen by the movie's co-star, Uggie the Jack Russell terrier, who delighted the crowd by standing on two legs and performing other tricks. (The film later won five Oscars.)

'Alas, poor Fido. I knew him well.'
18 January 2012

To mark the 150th anniversary of the London Underground,
Prince Charles and the Duchess of Cornwall travelled from
Farringdon to King's Cross (one stop) on the Metropolitan line.

'I don't understand. Charles and Camilla said it was quite jolly.'
1 February 2013

Thousands lined the route of Margaret Thatcher's cortège as it proceeded from the House of Commons through the streets of London to a lavish ceremonial funeral at St Paul's. Her husband Sir Denis Thatcher had died in 2003.

'Ah, Denis. Who was in charge up here – till now?'
17 April 2013

When the former England football captain, David Beckham OBE – renowned for his many body tattoos – finally retired, many were disappointed that he did not receive a knighthood in the New Year's Honours List for his work as an ambassador for the 2012 London Olympics.

'I'm disappointed David Beckham's not on the list – I was hoping to show him my new tattoo.'
31 December 2013

A study by scientists at the University of Oslo, Norway, claimed that giant central Asian gerbils were most likely to be responsible for bringing the Black Death plague to medieval Europe, not rats as previously thought.

'Oh, God! Run for it, Edith. I think we've got gerbils!'
25 February 2015

'Jagger', a three-year-old prize-winning Irish setter, died after being poisoned at Crufts dog show at the NEC in Birmingham. At least six other dogs that took part in the show were also believed to have been poisoned.

'You heard me, copper. He's saying nothing till his lawyer arrives!'
10 March 2015

In a sensational and historic general election vote, the Scottish National Party won 56 of the 59 seats in Scotland, making it the third largest party in the Westminster Parliament.

'I might be able to manage the haggis but I'm not sure I can cope with the deep-fried Mars bars.'

12 May 2015

The full text of a number of secret letters sent by Prince Charles to ministers in various UK Government departments in 2004 and 2005 were released after a 10-year battle by the *Guardian*. They were known as 'black spider notes' because of his spindly handwriting,

'. . . regarding your recent letter complaining about my rule and suggesting nice little retirement homes in Bournemouth – GET LOST! Yours affectionately, Mother.' *15 May 2015*

A *Sun* front-page headline 'Queen Backs Brexit', referring to alleged private comments attacking the EU made by Her Majesty, was deemed 'significantly misleading' by the Independent Press Standards Organisation.

'I assure you, William is not backing the EU. All members of the royal household are completely unbiased.'

18 February 2016

Following the successful campaign to charge for plastic carrier bags,
there was a call to ban non-recyclable takeaway coffee cups.

'I said: "Do you remember when it was plastic bags?" '
16 March 2016

The Government confirmed that it would back a scheme to set up
Britain's first spaceport to launch satellites and tourists into orbit.
One of the leading contenders for the site was Newquay in Cornwall.

'I'm just popping out, m'dear. Is there anything you want in Australia?'

19 May 2016

The nation went to the polls to vote in the Referendum on whether to Leave or Remain in the European Union. In the event the Leave voters won by 52 per cent to 48 per cent.

'It's crunch day, Philip. The nation decides who's in charge – me or Mrs Merkel.'

23 June 2016

Following the resignation of David Cameron, former Home Secretary Theresa May was elected the new leader of the Conservative Party and became Britain's second female Prime Minister (after Margaret Thatcher).

'Yes, go on, Margaret . . . Buy a really big handbag . . . Then what?'

6 July 2016

It was reported that two police forces in the South West of England had set up Britain's first operational drone squad to fight crime. The drones, equipped with day- and night-vision cameras, would help with missing person searches, road traffic collisions and crime scene photography.

'Are you absolutely sure it's only a police drone? It's just incinerated Woofums!'

21 March 2017

In an attempt to combat the shortage of beds in NHS hospitals, a pilot Airbnb-style scheme was introduced in Essex which offered members of the public up to £1000 a month to let their spare rooms to patients recovering from surgery.

'I thought you'd be pleased. We are getting £1000 a month!'

27 October 2017

On 27 November 2017, Clarence House announced that Prince Harry would marry the US actress Meghan Markle in the spring of 2018. They were engaged earlier the same month in London.

'MARKLE, Philip, dear. MEGHAN MARKLE! Harry's not marrying Angela Merkel!'

28 November 2017

Ingvar Kamprad, the Swedish billionaire founder of IKEA, which pioneered flat-pack self-assembly furniture, died aged 91.

'I believe he was the creator of IKEA.'

30 January 2018

During French President Emmanuel Macron's three-day state visit to the USA – the first by a foreign leader since Donald Trump took office – the two heads of state struck up an unexpectedly warm friendship.

'I don't know how we're going to break this to the wives. Trump and Macron have eloped!

26 April 2018

In the run-up to the royal wedding there was much speculation about who would be invited from Meghan Markle's family. In the event her mother was the only close relative to attend as her father was unable to make it due to a heart operation.

'He says he's the second cousin of Hollerin' Hank Markle from Nashville and he's here to duet with you on Saturday.' *17 May 2018*